Collins

Learn to Paint

Coastal Landscapes

Ray Balkwill

In memory of my father-in-law, Terry, who shared my
love of boats and water.

First published in 2006 by
Collins, an imprint of
HarperCollins*Publishers*
77-85 Fulham Palace Road
Hammersmith, London W6 8JB

The Collins website address is:
www.collins.co.uk

Collins is a registered trademark of HarperCollins Publishers Limited.

07 09 11 10 08 06
2 4 6 8 7 5 3 1

© Ray Balkwill 2006

Ray Balkwill asserts the moral right to be identified as the author of this work.

A catalogue record for this book is available from the British Library.

Editor: Diana Vowles
Designer: Caroline Hill
Photographer: Nigel Cheffers-Heard

ISBN-13 978 0 00 717559 8
ISBN-10 0 00 717559 0

Colour reproduction by Colourscan, Singapore
Printed and bound by Printing Express Ltd, Hong Kong

Previous page: **Restless Sea** *mixed media* 34 x 49.5 cm (13½ x 19½ in)
This page: **Sketch** *watercolour* 10 x 13 cm (4 x 5 in)
Opposite: **Summer Haze, St Ives** *mixed media* 43 x 48 cm (17 x 19 in)

Contents

Portrait of an Artist

Ray Balkwill was born in 1948 in Exeter, Devon. He enjoyed drawing from a very early age and making a career in art was always his ambition. However, it was not fine art but graphic design that he first studied at Exeter College of Art. When Ray graduated from college he worked as a designer in advertising agencies, firstly in London and then in the West Country. The turning point came in 1985 when he decided to pick up painting again alongside his main occupation as an art director. Demand for his paintings soon grew and resulted in him turning professional in 1990.

Since then his work has been shown in galleries all over the UK, and he has had numerous solo and joint exhibitions. Ray's work has also been hung in major open exhibitions including those of the Royal Institute of Painters in Watercolour, the Royal West of England Academy and the South West Academy of Fine and Applied Arts. In 1999 he was elected a member of the St Ives Society of Artists. He holds regular exhibitions in his spacious studio gallery at his home in Exmouth, giving the public an opportunity to view some of his latest work and, from time to time, the work of other invited artists.

Sharing his knowledge

Ray has also built up a considerable reputation as a teacher; he runs painting holidays from his Devon studio, in Cornwall and occasionally overseas. He also gives lectures, demonstrations and workshops to art groups throughout the West Country. Painting can be a solitary occupation, so Ray enjoys sharing his experiences with fellow artists and finds the whole process of teaching necessary and very rewarding.

Ray is a regular contributor to *The Artist* magazine and his work has also featured in *International Artist* and *Pastel Artist International*. He is the author of two books and his work appears in many other publications. An art instruction film of him painting on the Exe estuary has also been made by APV Films. He is a strong advocate of painting *en plein air* and his main objective is always to capture the mood and spirit of a place. Living as he does on the coast, it is little wonder that the forces of nature and the wide-open spaces of sea and sky have been the mainspring of his art.

▲ Ray Balkwill sketching on the Exe estuary.

▶ **Sunlit Water, Topsham**
watercolour
35 x 25 cm (14 x 10 in)
The soft, hazy light inspired this painting of the Exe estuary and watercolour was the perfect choice for capturing it.

Introduction

Whether there are thundering windswept waves crashing onto rugged rocks or the reflections of a glorious sunset in a gentle swell, the coastal landscape inspires within me the creative need to capture these emotional moments in paint. I am drawn to water in all its many guises. After all, there are a thousand and one things to stir the imagination: the ever-changing light, boats of all shapes and sizes, big skies, reflections, tide-pools and rusting chains to name but a few. It's not only a visual feast, either – the sound of crashing waves, the 'popping' mud on a falling tide, the cries of the gulls and the smell of seaweed combine to make the coast one of the most inspirational subjects to paint.

I believe the starting point for any good painting is to have a passion for the subject. It is about your personal as well as physical relationship with the landscape, which artists call 'a sense of place'. Combine this with keen observational skills and a sound technique and your goal of producing work you are pleased with is in sight. However, there are no shortcuts to painting successful coastal landscapes – it starts with sketching, as often as you can. Drawing sets down the ideas and memory of an experience, thinking ahead to the finished painting.

▲ **Reflections, Otter Head**
mixed media
34 x 47 cm
(13½ x 18½ in)
In art, expressiveness counts far more than photographic accuracy and working on location rather than in the studio encourages this.

How this book can help

This book covers a variety of my favourite subjects, including seascapes, still water and the reflections within it, skies, estuaries, boats and harbours. The comprehensive materials section covers the drawing and painting materials that I use, including watercolour, gouache, pastels, mixed media and oils. The different ways of approaching subjects are suggested along with examples of the techniques you might use, and the step-by-step demonstrations take you through complete projects to show you the development of a painting from start to finish.

Whatever your level of ability may be, my hope is that through my words and paintings you will find further ideas and inspiration which will help you in the development of your own individual approach to painting coastal landscapes. Of course, learning to paint in a way to express your true self doesn't always come naturally, or immediately. But one thing is certain; your artistic journey will always be an exciting one. Bon voyage!

◀ **Down to the Bay**
oils
23 x 36 cm (9 x 14 in)
A prepared mid-tone board gave this quick sketch an overall unity by letting the ground colour show through.

▼ **Bright Day, St Ives**
mixed media
33 x 45 cm (13 x 18 in)
Every landscape must be expressed with its own feeling, its own atmosphere and light. St Ives in Cornwall is noted for its clarity of light and it was this that was the inspiration behind the painting.

Choosing a Medium

The materials you choose will vary depending upon your intentions and you may have already developed your own preferences. However, it is worth considering here the merits of one medium over another. Of course, this is by no means a comprehensive guide, but more my own personal choice of materials and equipment.

Sketching

There is an enormous range of drawing materials available today, from felt-tip and steel-nib dip pens to graphite and water-soluble pencils of all descriptions. It is worth exploring the potential of as many different types as possible. I find solid graphite pencils (2B and 4B) are ideal for drawing and I also enjoy the effects water-soluble watercolour pencils can give, particularly when I want a quick tonal sketch of a sky, for instance.

Willow charcoal is another responsive medium and is available in sticks of varying thickness, as well as in pencil form. I also combine my charcoal drawings with black and white Conté pencils or crayons, as well as felt-tip pens.

When it comes to permanent or water-soluble felt-tip pens, there is a wide range of tips to give every conceivable mark that you could wish for. Remember, though, that many of these pens are unlikely to be lightfast, so you may have to do some tests. I use an A3 cartridge pad (135 gsm/140 lb weight) for my charcoal sketches and smaller hardback sketchbooks for my pencil and watercolour studies. There are many different sizes available to choose from, but my own preference is for a landscape format of approximately 23 x 30 cm (9 x 12 in). Other useful equipment includes a hard eraser, putty eraser, craft knife and a can of spray fixative.

▲ From top to bottom: Putty eraser, water-soluble felt-tip brush pen, permanent felt-tip pens, water-soluble pencils, willow charcoal, Conté crayons, charcoal pencil, solid graphite pencils and art pen.

Watercolour

Watercolour is still the most popular medium used by artists, despite its being the most difficult to master. This is partly due to it being such a portable medium and ideal for working on location. However, I find its characteristics of translucency, expressiveness and unpredictability make it by far the most exciting medium to use.

I put watercolour paper at the top of my list of priorities when it comes to materials, as I have found that choosing the right paper is the most important step towards improvement. There is a wide choice available, so I suggest experimenting with the many different types until you find your favourites. My own preferences include Whatman, Saunders and Arche. The surface I prefer is either Not or Rough, depending on the subject, usually in a 300 gsm (140 lb) weight. This is stretched onto a drawing board using a gummed brown-paper tape. I also use two sizes of drawing boards, 56 x 66 cm (22 x 30 in) and 41 x 58 cm (16 x 23 in), which accommodate a quarter and a half imperial sheet of watercolour paper respectively.

Brushes come in a variety of shapes, sizes and quality from synthetics to the more expensive sable. My own choice includes a 25 mm (1 in) hake, a round (No. 12) synthetic-sable mix, a filbert (No. 14) and a rigger (No. 1).

I prefer to use tubes of Artists' quality paint, rather than pans. Colours are squeezed out into my paint-box, or onto a large plastic palette and several porcelain plates. My palette consists of: Cadmium Red, Permanent Rose, Light Red, Burnt Umber, Burnt Sienna, Raw Sienna, French Ultramarine, Coeruleum, Cobalt Blue, Phthalo Blue (Red Shade), Cadmium Yellow, Lemon Yellow, Naples Yellow and Cadmium Orange. Additional useful colours include Viridian and Indigo.

Other items include a ruler, kitchen roll, art masking fluid, sponge, roll of masking tape and, when working on location, a small plastic bottle of water and a collapsible lantern water pot.

▼ Shown here are my basic materials for working in watercolour.

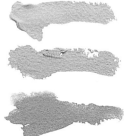

▲ Gouache colours, clockwise from top right: Flesh Tint, Brown Pink, Permanent White, Cool Grey, Warm Grey and Naples Yellow.

Soft pastel

The equipment needed for painting in pastel is conveniently light and portable and the immediacy of the medium lends itself perfectly to a direct response, without the problems of paint drying too fast or too slowly or colour mixing on the palette. There is an excellent choice of soft pastels available today, with each manufacturer producing a wide range of tints and shades, as well as different shapes and sizes. My own pastel box is made up of colours from all the well-known brands. I also employ some harder pastels such as pastel pencils and Conté crayons, which are ideal for adding detail to a painting.

▼ **The Twelve Bens from Lettermore, Connemara**
pastel
27 x 37 cm
(10½ x 14½ in)
This painting was done on a warm mid-tone pastel paper, which you can see in the foreground. This paper is useful for landscape, particularly if the colour is left to show through in the final picture.

▲ Materials I use for painting in gouache.

Gouache

Gouache is a versatile medium in its own right and can give a vibrancy and energetic quality to a painting. However, I use it combined with watercolours for my location studies. It is more opaque than watercolour and dries to a slightly chalky matt finish. Gouache can be combined with watercolour to great effect, to give highlights, contrast and solidity. It can also be thinned with water to a fluid consistency.

Because gouache is an opaque medium the translucency of white paper is not as important as with watercolour, so it is suitable for a wide variety of supports. My own choice is Canson Mi-Teintes pastel paper, which I stretch with gummed brown-paper tape. As it is a water-based medium, the same watercolour brushes can also be used. There is a wide range of gouache colours to choose from, but shown above are a few that I find useful.

Supports vary from pastel papers to boards and glass-paper. The texture or 'tooth' of the support is an important consideration, as well as its colour and tonal value. My own preference is to use tinted pastel papers, or watercolour papers (Not surface) if combining with watercolour. I do not fix my pastels, as it tends to darken the lighter colours, but there are no hard and fast rules about this – in fact I know many artists who spray while their painting is in progress, but often leave the top layer unsprayed. Transporting paintings can be a problem, particularly those that have been done on location. However, I simply tape a piece of newspaper over the painting in order to protect it and prevent any movement.

When working on location my selection of colours is reduced considerably and contained in a few small boxes. Other useful additions include a container of ground rice for cleaning the pastels, tissues for blending and a bristle brush for correcting mistakes. I recommend that you not only remove the labels from your pastels, but also make a colour chart with reference numbers alongside the colours. You will find this especially invaluable when it comes to renewing your favourite colours.

▲ Keeping pastels in separate compartments makes it easy to find the colour you need and prevents them picking up dust from other colours.

▲ Because there is such a wide range of tints and shades to choose from, a good starting point is to select a light, medium and dark pastel from each colour range.

Oils

The smooth, buttery consistency of oils gives the medium a sensual richness which is unlike any other. When painting on location I use a box easel that carries everything I need. The supports I use vary from a medium-tooth stretched canvas to my own prepared boards. For these I use MDF (Medium Density Fibreboard) or hardboard, which I prime with two coats of gesso and then a final coat mixed with an equal amount of texture paste. This gives the surface an interesting texture on which to work. The sizes vary, but my preference is 35 x 25 cm (14 x 10 in) and 35 x 35cm (14 x 14 in). I prefer softer nylon brushes to the traditional bristle brushes, but whichever you use the important thing is to have a variety of shapes and sizes.

I choose Artists' as well as Georgian Oil Colours and find 38 ml tubes the most practical size except in the case of Titanium White, which I buy in 115 ml tubes. My standard palette colours are shown below; additional useful colours include Cadmium Lemon Yellow, Cobalt Violet, Cadmium Orange, Light Red and Burnt Umber. I use Genuine Turpentine as a solvent to mix the colours and clean the brushes with white spirit.

I mix my pigments on a traditional mahogany palette and lay out my colours as shown here, with the warm colours grouped on one side and the cool colours on the other. Try to get in the habit of laying out your colours in the same order each time you paint, as this will save you valuable time and prevent you becoming distracted from your picture. Useful additions include a palette knife and, of course, plenty of clean rags and a bar of soap for cleaning brushes.

▲ Shown here are my basic materials for painting in oils.

◄ Oils from left to right: Titanium White, Viridian, Cadmium Yellow, Naples Yellow, Cadmium Red, Rose Madder, Coeruleum, French Ultramarine, Burnt Sienna and Raw Sienna.

Mixed media

Experimenting and combining media is something that I enjoy and I strongly recommend you try it. In particular, I find the combination of watercolour and soft pastel exciting and you will see many examples of this technique throughout the book. For this I use watercolour papers, which include Bockingford, Arche and Fabriano (Not). Some artists combine acrylics, gouache, inks and collage with drawing media as a means of extending their range of expression. I sometimes use acrylic and oils together, applying the quick-drying acrylics for the underpainting. I believe there are few rules in painting, but this is an important one: acrylics should never be put on top of oils, as they will crack.

When using mixed media, the combinations are endless and it is the great diversity of effects that intrigues me. Whatever materials you choose for the process of picture-making, one thing is for sure – they could lead you in a completely new direction for your work.

▲ **Sunlit Creek, Salcombe**
mixed media
33 x 46 cm (13 x 18 in)
The transparency of watercolour combined with the opacity and vibrancy of pastel work extremely well together, as this *plein air* painting shows. The white paper plays a crucial role in creating the sunlit water.

▼ Here is the equipment that I use whenever I am painting on location, which also includes my box easel for working in oils.

Outdoor painting equipment

Additional equipment for painting on location includes a simple viewfinder, which I find invaluable, as well as a lightweight sketching easel and folding stool. I have a shoulder bag for carrying all my materials, which can also be hung onto the easel to stabilize it during blustery weather conditions. I use a zipped folio case to carry my stool, drawing board and sketchbooks and when I am standing at the easel the case makes a useful table for materials, placed on the stool.

All artists have their own favourite materials and approach, but whatever medium you choose, travelling light is an important factor when working on location. 'Keeping it simple' not only applies to materials, but just about every other aspect of the painting process as well.

The Sketchbook

Sometimes we have to work hard to be inspired and to find that emotional tie between the subject and our heart. Turner once said: 'Painting is one per cent inspiration and ninety-nine per cent perspiration.' That first initial response between you and the subject is so important. Being 'moved' is the starting point – the spark that will ignite the fire. Then it's just a case of putting the first pencil mark down!

Drawing and understanding

A sketchbook can not only be used to gather information, allowing you to reconnect with the subject, but can also help you to understand the subject better. An artist's sketchbook is all about individual interpretation so it can take on many different forms, including that of a scrapbook, in which photographs, 'found' material and experiments are collated to help provide ideas and inspiration. I particularly enjoy looking at other artists' sketchbooks and seeing their working methods.

Perhaps most importantly, a sketchbook gives you the opportunity to practise and improve your drawing and observational skills. Drawing can be done, of course, just for the pure enjoyment it brings, with no finished work in mind. Painting is simply drawing with a brush, so every sketch you make will improve your skills as an artist.

When sketching, consider which medium is best for the subject you are recording, with particular regard to the time available

▼ For sketching I use an A3 cartridge pad and a pocket hardback sketchbook.

and what you wish to achieve. My own type of drawing can be broken down into two basic types – information sketches and atmosphere sketches.

Information sketches

This type of sketch is about gathering as much information as possible from the scene to act as an aide-memoire. They tend to be more carefully observed drawings done in graphite pencil, such as the one shown right. When I want a colour reference I add watercolour washes. However, to gather even more colour information, I use watercolour and gouache on a mid-tone tinted pastel paper. I call these 'location studies'. Examples are shown overleaf.

Atmosphere sketches

Quick impressions sketched in monochrome play a vital role in exploring tonal relationships and mood. I like to use a broad medium for this such as willow charcoal. These sketches

tend to be done quite quickly and I sometimes accompany them with written notes to remind me of the colours present. Water-soluble pencils and pens are a useful addition for quick tonal studies. A small box of carefully selected pastels can also be helpful for capturing skies and those fleeting moments of light.

▲ For drawing I prefer to use a 4B solid graphite pencil which, when applied on its side, can produce broader tonal marks as shown in this information sketch.

◄ For this atmosphere sketch a felt-tip pen was used to do the drawing and then charcoal was added to achieve the subtle tones. For the texture of the foreground beach, I used a Conté crayon applied on its side.

▶ This quick sketch of a wide expanse of sea, sky and estuary was painted in gouache on a warm, mid-tone pastel paper.

Sketch to finished painting

Every painter works differently, some working more confidently back in the studio from their sketches, while others enjoy painting on location. I am one of those artists who prefer to work *en plein air* as much as possible. The challenges of different weather conditions and constantly changing light seem to make me work more quickly and intuitively than when I am working in the studio. Here I find my paintings sometimes get overworked and knowing when to stop can be a real problem – even for a professional artist! To try to overcome this I set myself a maximum time limit of two to three hours, working as much as possible from my

▼ I often sketch with pencil and wash, using both sides of a hardback sketchbook. The colours at Talland Bay fascinate me, particularly the myriad purple, pinks and greens to be found in the rocks here.

16

Quick impressions sketched in monochrome can play a vital role in exploring tonal relationships, mood and composition. Here are just a few examples of such atmosphere sketches. Top to bottom: solid graphite pencil, water-soluble pencil (Indigo), and felt-tip pen and gouache on a tinted pastel paper.

sketches, backed up if necessary with photographs. When I am working on location I paint to this same time limit if possible, as there are only a few hours before the light changes dramatically.

Working from photographs

Photographs are a useful backup for any artist, particularly when recording subjects in motion such as breaking waves, a dramatic sky, or even the fishing boat you are painting which is about to leave the harbour! When working from colour photographs defining tonal values can be difficult, so it is helpful to photocopy them in black and white. This is where the digital camera and computer can also be another useful tool for the artist.

However, do not become over-reliant on your photographic references at the cost of your sketchbook; the problem is that they show far too much detail and the colours can be misleading. The photograph can never be a substitute for looking hard at the subject and rekindling those initial feelings in the same way a sketch can.

Skies and Weather

The master painter of skies John Constable once said: 'That landscape painter who does not make his skies a very material part of his composition neglects to avail himself of one of his greatest aids.' The sky provides an endless source of material for the artist and is one of the most important elements in a landscape, as it sets the mood for the whole painting. For instance, think how often we see cloud shadows moving across the landscape, or being reflected in a river or lake. In seascapes too, the sky is not only reflected in the sea and wet sand, but also affects the way light touches the surface of the sea.

You don't have to be a meteorologist to paint convincing skies, though it does help to have a basic understanding of the different types of cloud formations and the weather they bring. Remember though that painting skies relies on two important factors: keen observation and memory.

Spontaneity and simplicity

Clouds are constantly on the move, so this means you have to work extremely quickly to capture those fleeting moments. Therefore, the size you work and the medium you choose are both important factors to consider. Before working in colour, seeing skies tonally in monochrome is a good place to start. Use a broad medium such as charcoal, which is without equal for rendering a variety of interesting marks from sensitive line to rapid areas of broad tone. The lighter areas can then be lifted out with a kneaded eraser, or added with a white Conté crayon.

If you have difficulty in seeing the tonal values in a sky, you may find it helpful to view it in what is known as a Claude mirror.

▲ In this very quick charcoal and felt-tip pen sketch the whites for the clouds were both lifted out with a putty eraser and added in with the use of white Conté crayon.

▼ Working wet-into-wet is an expressive watercolour technique, perfect for skies. Colour can be applied onto damp paper, or directly into wet paint, which produces beautiful soft, diffused shapes. Here French Ultramarine was merged with Naples Yellow and a mix of Coeruleum and Permanent Rose was dropped into the wet wash.

◄ Gouache, combined with watercolour, is a favourite medium for painting quick studies of skies. The paper used here is a Canson Mi-Teinte paper (colour Moonstone) with a combination of both thick and diluted gouache with some watercolour added. The clouds were softened as they receded by adding a touch of Naples Yellow to the white gouache.

Paint a piece of smooth, clear glass on one side with black acrylic paint to make the mirror. Hold it in front of you and you will see the sky behind you reflected in it. The reflection in this darker surface can be surprising and quite ordinary scenes can reveal themselves as excellent subjects, particularly skies. Alternatively, you can use a piece of black perspex or just wear a pair of dark sunglasses.

Each medium has its own qualities in capturing the transient effects of skies, but my favourite has to be watercolour.

▲ Because there is no colour mixing needed, pastel lends itself to painting skies quickly. If you allow the colour and tone of the paper to show through in some areas it will add subtle variations of colour to cloud formations, as shown here. Choosing the right colour and tone of paper is very important. If you choose a paper that is either too dark or too light you will always be fighting against it.

If you have a busy landscape you should keep the sky simple and vice versa.

**▲ A Good Day
for Sailing**
oils
25 x 36 cm (10 x14 in)
The immense Exe
estuary sky was also
reflected in the water
and it was this light
and atmosphere that
was the inspiration for
the painting. It is
painted thinly with oils,
allowing the coloured
ground to play an
important role in the
overall harmony of
the painting.

Soft, transparent washes are ideal for
suggesting cumulus clouds, stormy skies,
and in particular mist or fog. Keep the
water container brim-full as you will find
it easier to gauge how far the brush is being
immersed and therefore how much water
it is holding without taking your attention
away from your painting too much.

Being bold

Be sure to be bold with watercolour, paint
with expression and take risks – this after
all is the essence of the medium. Often
mistakes and accidents can form an
integral part of the picture. When painting

skies, is also useful to hold the brush as
lightly as possible, working with your
whole arm rather than just from the wrist.
A good tip is to have a dry run with a brush
to get a feel for the way the paint will
be applied.

Gouache too is a versatile medium for
portraying skies, particularly when
combined with watercolour and used on
a tinted support. Opaque gouache acts
more like oil paint, but I often use it in both
a transparent and opaque way within the
same painting. I suggest you do not use
white for clouds straight from the tube, but
rather tint it with another colour. This rule
also applies when working in oils.

▶ **Sailing Weather, Dartmouth**
watercolour
25 x 36 cm (10 x 14 in)
Watercolour techniques of layered washes as well as wet-into-wet have been used in this painting to suggest soft, diffuse effects in the changeable sky.

Oil paint lends itself beautifully to the subject, particularly for stormy skies or great billowing clouds. Soft pastel is also useful for painting skies as there is no colour mixing required, which of course saves valuable time when you are working on location – an important consideration if you are painting a sunset, for instance. When painting skies in pastel I like to use a combination of strokes, from blending to the firmer, more direct marks with the pastel used on its side.

◀ **Evening Sky, Exmouth**
pastel
37 x 55 cm
(14½ x 21½ in)
This painting was done on a mid-tone pastel paper with the initial drawing put in with a felt-tip pen. Perspective applies to clouds, those nearest being larger and contrasting more in tone than those further away. Note how blue sky becomes cooler and lighter towards the horizon.

Estuaries

O ver many years I have painted almost
every estuary in the West Country. The
Exe, being on my doorstep, is still my
favourite, but each one is different in its light,
mood and colours. Painting at the river's edge
is a real joy, and a subject of which I never
tire. What makes it so exciting for me is the
ever-changing source of material as the tide
sweeps in and out, continually casting a new
aspect on both land and water. Watercolour
is perhaps the ideal medium as its essence of
translucency and expressiveness lends itself
beautifully to painting both sky and water.

Thoughtful planning

Although the transient effects of sky and water
lend themselves to painting in watercolour,
the unpredictability of the medium means
that much forward planning is necessary
as mistakes cannot be easily remedied.
Nevertheless, despite its difficulties, I still find
it the most exciting medium to use and when
it works it's magical.

While estuaries make a far prettier
sight when the tide is in, it is at low tide
that I find the subject most inspiring.

▲ **Morning Flight
Over the Exe Estuary**
watercolour
25 x 36 cm (10 x 14 in)
Here the reserved
highlights of the white
paper contrasted with
the soft wet-into-wet
washes and the texture
created by dry-brush
technique give a
unique atmosphere
and mood of which
only this medium
is capable.

The contrasts and textures of sand, wet mud, tide-pools and water give far more possibilities for an interesting composition. The subject also lends itself to combining watercolour and pastel in a mixed media painting in order to fully exploit these contrasts and textures. The transparency and fluidity of watercolour and the opacity and vibrancy of pastel work extremely well together.

Still water and reflections

Whichever medium you choose, in achieving wet-looking water you will need to keep your painting technique simple. Watercolour is the most obvious choice and often a few sweeping brush strokes on damp paper can give an instant impression of still water. However, opaque mediums such as gouache, oils and pastels can also be equally suggestive if simply painted.

The essential characteristic of still water is that it reflects the sky and whatever is close to it in the landscape. Water that is nearer to you always appears darker, as the depth of the water or the ground underneath is the predominant influence on tone and colour. Remember, too, that reflections always have less intensity of both colour and tone than the objects they mirror. A reflection of a dark boat, for instance, will be reflected lighter and vice versa. An object that stands upright in the water produces a reflection of the same length, but if the object leans towards you then it will appear longer. If the object is leaning away from you then the reflection appears shorter.

When the surface of the water is disturbed, reflections break up and appear longer than the reflected object. These broken reflections too follow the laws of perspective. As they recede into the distance they gradually appear smaller, flatter and more closely spaced.

◀ **Passing Shower, Topsham**
mixed media
43 x 43 cm (17 x 17 in)
Tranquillity was the inspiration here and the translucent washes of watercolour add to this feeling. A small amount of pastel was added discerningly to create texture and contrast. It is important not to apply too much pressure on the brush when painting in watercolour. I always liken the correct handling to the brush 'dancing' on the paper.

23

▲ **Morning Mist**
watercolour
13 x 18 cm (5 x 7 in)
This atmospheric
painting of the Yealm
estuary in Devon shows
to good effect a
number of the classic
watercolour techniques.

Painting water and foreshore

When I am painting estuaries, the wide
variety of pattern, texture and colour to be
found in sand and wet mud never ceases to
amaze me. Sound observation will soon show
you that the textural world around you can
be very exciting in its unexpectedness. Of
course there are many ways of painting water
and foreshore, but over the next few pages

you will find just a few examples of the
techniques that I employ with each medium.

   Be careful not to overwork a technique,
as it could easily make the painting too
contrived and gimmicky. There are also many
products available to help you achieve effects,
but my advice is to use these with discretion.
However, there are no hard and fast rules and
almost endless ways of applying paint to
paper, so it is worth experimenting to achieve
the effects you require.

Watercolour techniques

Watercolour's unpredictability and the
random effects that can be achieved with it
are part of its charm. A few classic techniques
are described here to give you a starting point
from which to explore further.

When painting
in watercolour, use
a large container of water and
be sure to refill it regularly.

Wet-into-wet

This is the perfect technique for suggesting water and reflections. When watercolour is applied to either damp paper or wet paint it merges to give a soft and hazy effect.

Dry brush

As its name implies, this technique uses a minimum of paint direct from the tube to create a broken colour when applied to a Not or Rough surfaced paper. The paint catches the tooth of the paper, creating a textured effect with economy by a simple brushstroke. I often soften edges by painting over some areas with water. Dry brush is also useful for creating a sparkle on water with white gouache.

Masking fluid

This liquid latex is useful to reserve highlights, particularly when you need to lay a wash over a large area. When it is applied with an old brush to a Not or Rough watercolour paper, the tooth of the paper can be used to good effect to produce texture which will suggest wet, glistening mud, for instance. When the masking fluid is dry it can be removed by rubbing off with a finger.

Granulation

This can produce a subtle grainy texture to a wash, which is useful when placed deliberately in a painting to make large areas more interesting. Certain watercolour pigments have a tendency to granulate (manufacturers' charts will guide you here), but you can also buy a granulation medium for this purpose.

Spattering

Flicking or spattering paint onto a support is an effective way of suggesting stones, pebbles and textures in sand. This can be done onto dry or damp paper, giving the two completely different effects shown here. For this I used a bristle brush, but for a slightly denser spatter, I tap a loaded brush across the handle of another brush.

▶ **On the Yealm Estuary**
pastel
37 x 55 cm
(14½ x 21½ in)
Blended pastels are the perfect medium for sky and water, as this painting shows. The strong horizontal strokes in the water also impart a feeling of tranquillity to the scene.

Pastel techniques

Although pastels are an opaque medium, similar effects to watercolour can be achieved. It is the choice of support that is the main difference between the two. Pastels can of course be applied to any surface, but when you are painting in pastels tinted papers or boards are the traditional support. Careful consideration of the texture, colour and tonal value of the support is vital.

When you are painting water you may think of choosing a blue or grey paper because of the amount of the colour present in the scene. However, I find the warmer colours – in particular the mid-toned pinks, umbers and browns – work better. This enables me to apply the contrasting blues with pastel. Like the colour of the paper, the tone has considerable importance and generally, a light-toned paper emphasizes the dark colours in a painting. For dramatic contrasts of light and dark, try using light colours on a dark paper.

Blending pastel

This technique is perfect for suggesting water as colours can be softened by gently blending with a finger, or, for larger areas, with the side of your hand. For a softer effect I use a tissue, which tends to lift some of the pastel off the support. Pastels can of course also be blended together on the support to make additional colours.

Softening pastel with water

Pastel can also be blended with water to give a softer effect that is ideal for portraying water. Moving pastel around with water is a good way of simplifying a complicated area in a painting. It also enables you to build up further layers of pastel without disturbing the colour underneath.

Broken colour with soft pastel

When the pastel is applied on its side across a textured support it will adhere to the raised tooth of the paper and miss the hollows. This mark is perfect for suggesting texture for mud and beaches. The effect of broken colour allows other colours beneath it to show through – particularly useful when working in watercolour and pastel combined. For harder marks and greater control of handling I use Conté crayons as well as pastel pencils.

Scumbling

Scumbling can not only give an interesting surface texture but also create subtle colour effects. Loose circular strokes are lightly applied to create a thin veil of colour that does not entirely cover the one beneath. A number of layers can be built up in this way to give depth to your colours as well as unifying areas of your painting.

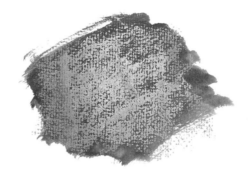

▼ **Awaiting the Tide, La Forêt-Fouesnant, Brittany**
mixed media
33 x 51 cm (13 x 20 in)
This painting had to be done fast as the tide would soon change the whole scene. The transparency of watercolour and the opacity of pastel work well together. Notice how the tide-pools aid the composition by helping to lead your eye to the focal point.

Gouache techniques

Gouache is a versatile and often underrated medium that can be combined with watercolour to produce a variety of interesting effects. Working on a tinted support, such as pastel paper or mountboard, considerably extends the artist's scope for expression.

Light over dark

The main advantages of painting with gouache is that light colours can be painted over dark, in a way similar to oil painting. The covering power of gouache also enables you to rescue a watercolour painting more easily. The intense colours of gouache means that its inclusion with watercolour can highlight any area you wish to be a focal point. Using the dry-brush technique and white gouache straight from the tube is a useful way to suggest sparkling sunlit water.

Thinning with water

Thinning white gouache with varying quantities of water gives it a semi-opaque, 'milky' quality, which is useful for suggesting the transparent qualities in skies and water. I sometimes add touches of watercolour to the gouache to soften the harshness of the white further.

▼ **Evening Sky, Topsham**
watercolour and gouache
25 x 36 cm (10 x 14 in)
Thinned white gouache, softened in places with small touches of watercolour, brings an element of transparency to the sky and water in this painting.

◄ **Cleaning the Nets, Lympstone**
oils
25 x 36 cm (10 x 14 in)
Gesso was used in this painting to give textural surface, while runs of turpentine wash produced some of the texture seen in the reflections and buildings.

Oil techniques

With oils I always work on a toned ground, usually staining the board with a warm sienna, umber or brown. If the colour of the ground is allowed to show through it acts as a unifying element in the finished painting. The compositional main shapes are then blocked in with a thin and fast-drying darker colour, usually French Ultramarine and Burnt Sienna. This underpainting not only provides a foundation from which the painting can be developed further, but can also form the basis for a number of textural techniques. I work on the principle of 'fat-over-lean', and like to work with thick and thin paint to create different effects. When I am portraying water I try to suggest it by using the paint as thinly as possible.

Gesso underpainting

Acrylic gesso applied to a support with a brush can give an interesting textural surface to oil paint applied once it has dried (see the detail from *Cleaning the Nets, Lympstone*, right). An equal mix of texture paste can also be added to the gesso to give an even more pronounced texture. Gesso can be used on varying supports to give texture for watercolour, pastels and acrylics.

Thinning with turpentine

By painting turpentine or white spirit into oil paint already applied to the support you can achieve some exciting effects, as the detail from *Cleaning the Nets, Lympstone* shown right demonstrates. The board was first primed with gesso and texture paste and when this was dry the underpainting was blocked in with a 'turpentine wash' using French Ultramarine and Burnt Sienna. If you use this technique with the board held almost vertically the turpentine will run down to add extra texture. Leave this to dry for a short while before painting into it further.

▲ Gesso underpainting.

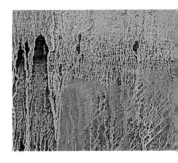

▲ Thinning with turpentine.

The Coastline

My painting trips have taken me to many different shores over the years, but it has been the Cornish coastline that has become a favourite theme for my more recent work. I find it an inexhaustible source of inspiration with its picturesque harbours, rugged coast and magical light. It is not difficult to understand why it has been a haunt for colonies of artists for hundreds of years.

For painting the power of the sea, oils have perhaps been the favoured medium, as many fine painters have proved over the centuries. One such artist, and in my opinion the finest, was Julius Olsson (1864–1942), who himself worked mainly in Cornwall. He once said: 'One whose heart draws him to the sea must, in the first place, have an exceptionally

▲ **Porthcothan**
water-soluble pen and charcoal
19 x 26 cm (7½ x 10 in)
I enjoy experimenting with different drawing and painting media. Here water-soluble felt-tip pen was combined with charcoal. Water was then added with a brush.

◄ This quick sketch uses both watercolour and gouache, a combination particularly useful for skies and cliffs.

30

▲ Treyarnon, North Cornwall
mixed media
33 x 51 cm (13 x 20 in)
This was one of those days when speed was of the essence as the tide was receding fast.

My inspiration here was the reflection of the distant headland. I helped cast this as my focal point by pulling the eye to it by way of the natural 'S' shape of the tide-pools.

▲ A quick and simple sketch done from a high viewpoint such as this can often make an exciting composition.

retentive memory, and be able to grasp in a few moments the effect of the ever-changing movements of the sea and sky; he must have a delicate and subtle sense of colour, and have the ability to place the main features of his impression of the subject on the canvas with few strokes of the brush, and, beside this, he must be prepared to face a brave fight with the elements, which will be frequently against him.'

His words describe my sentiments entirely, and whichever painting medium is chosen, a direct and bravura technique is required to bring the energy to the work which is so important.

Composition

This ever-changing subject can present you with a number of compositional difficulties, particularly if you are painting a view of the open sea, when the horizon where sea and sky meet will need to be carefully observed.

Creating a centre of interest in situations such as this can sometimes be a real problem and for isolating a specific area you will find a viewfinder indispensable. One solution here is to place the darkest dark next to the lightest light for the focal point, which can often be a wave crashing onto a rock. Swirling seagulls or a fishing boat out to sea can become an obvious focus of interest, but again careful consideration should be given to where these are placed.

Rocks, waves, foam patterns and clouds can be helpful in leading the eye to the main interest. You can control the mood of the picture by the way they are painted. They can be shown as a gentle and meandering 'S' movement, for instance, or by a strong and direct diagonal movement to add dynamism.

Waves

Painting waves can be a daunting subject, particularly for beginners. Recording what you see and feel is the key to painting them successfully. With keen observation and sound

▲ Sketching in pen and watercolour on cartridge paper gives a much crisper edge to the washes. This sketch was more about recording the colours in the rocks and sea than the waves themselves.

▼ **Waves at Talland Bay**
mixed media
36 x 53 cm (14 x 21 in)
Masking fluid was used in this painting to reserve the whites of the waves crashing on to the rocks.

drawing, you will soon see an overall design element emerging. I find that to capture the spirit of the sea, it is necessary to draw and paint as simply as possible with the minimum of marks in the direction and movement of the waves. Don't be hesitant; painting waves can bring out a freedom and perhaps a newly found expression in your work.

▼ This watercolour sketch was all about exploring contrast and shapes and developing tonal values.

Masking fluid is a useful medium, particularly for waves crashing onto rocks. I find that applying it with a large brush gives the best results, but use an old one, not your best sable! Clean it by scrubbing it into a bar of soap after use. Remember that when a wave strikes a rock the spray cast up is not as white as the bulk of the foam; it has more colours in it, influenced by the sky, rocks or shore. To suggest this I often soften the whiteness of the watercolour paper by applying pastel or gouache.

The sky plays a major influence upon the colours in the sea and you will need to observe these carefully. You will be surprised by just how many colours you actually see.

Capturing the movement

Sticks of willow charcoal are an excellent medium for capturing the movement of waves. Combining charcoal with white Conté crayon or soft white pastel on a mid-tone tinted pastel paper can also be helpful. Water-soluble pens and pencils are also useful for quick renderings and can be combined with other media too.

◄ Quick sketches in charcoal and white soft chalk pastel on tinted paper are an invaluable method of capturing the essentials of the subject. Sugar paper is an inexpensive alternative to pastel papers, but remember this is not lightfast.

▲ Figures immediately give life and scale to a scene, so sketch them at every opportunity. They will always be invaluable references for your paintings in the future.

those in the distance. Holding up a small piece of white card will help you see this more clearly.

The foreshore

The sandy shoreline of the coast is an inspiring place for the artist in search of painting material. Small-scale subjects such as rock pools, crabs, shells and driftwood can often be overlooked for the bigger picture, so remember to study what is beneath your feet.

Notice how the colours and tones of the sand change as waves recede. Wet sand will initially be light and reflective and will darken as the water seeps away. With pebble beaches simplification is the key word. Look for simple, large changes of tone to establish a sense of recession. The shoreline will give

Just as there is a recession of colour and tone in the landscape, so there is in waves. They recede in tone from the lightest light in the foreground, darkening slightly to

▶ **Summer Sea, Treyarnon**
mixed media
48 x 48 cm (19 x 19 in)
This painting was inspired by the deep contrasts of sunlight and shadow, particularly the colours in the shadow of the rock in the foreground. It simply stopped me in my tracks and had to be painted.

you the opportunity to paint the many facets of water, with both breaking waves and still-water tide-pools as the tide recedes.

Figures

The addition of figures immediately gives a feeling of movement and scale to the scene. However, because the viewer's eye will always be drawn to people in a picture, their placing is critical. It seldom works if they are put in as an afterthought. Figures are best added as simply as possible, but make sure they relate correctly in size to their surroundings. If your figures are the focal point you can emphasize them with the use of counterchange – a light figure against a dark rock, or a dark figure against a light area.

Headlands and rocks

I have long been fascinated by the interaction of sea and landscape, particularly when it is viewed from a high vantage point. It can

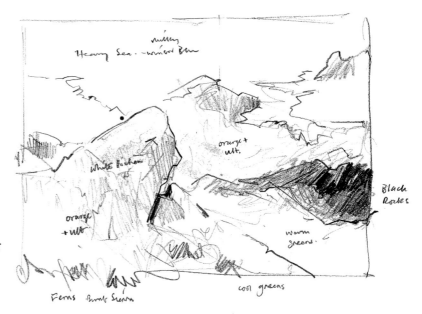

▲ Even a rapid sketch such as this encourages the analytical observation of things, which is a quite different process from just looking.

▼ **Rough Sea at Talland Bay**
mixed media
36 x 53 cm (14 x 21 in)
When it is anchored by more detailed background areas

a large foreground allows the artist a chance to explore some creative abstraction, as can be seen in the painting here.

provide you with a wide source of varied and interesting compositions.

Creating depth by using aerial perspective and contrasting colour temperatures plays a big part in coastal landscapes. You will find squinting at the scene or looking at it *contre-jour* (against the light) helpful as this defines three-dimensional forms and simplifies the main shapes. It is important to think in terms of masses and larger shapes rather than detail. Remember that shadows are not black but full of colour – something that is lost when working from photographs.

Observing tonal values

Colour, no matter how interesting, won't help if your rocks and headlands lack form or a feeling of solidity. When painting a rock, carefully observe its tonal values. The top of the rock is the lightest part as it receives the greatest amount of light; the vertical sides receive less light and the part facing away from the light source is the darkest area. When painting headlands a sunny day is helpful, as the shadows and strong contrast emphasize the dignity and atmosphere of form and distance more easily.

▲ **Towards Land's End from Cape Cornwall**
oils
33 x 23 cm (13 x 9 in)
When painting on location I use a box easel, which carries all that I need. It stands up to most weather conditions, although on this occasion it did blow over!

▶ **Rocks at Polperro**
mixed media
36 x 53 cm (14 x 21 in)
Watercolour and pastel are combined here to produce a painting of strong contrasts. The pastel was used to good effect in the suggestion of the spray and texture in the rocks.

◀ **Silver Sea, Talland Bay**
mixed media
53 x 36 cm (21 x 14 in)
With simplification and organization, a complex view from a high viewpoint such as this can make an exciting composition. Notice how I have placed the waves, the high-key area of the painting, in the Golden Section to create the focal point. To accentuate this further, a few swirling seagulls were also added. Stronger and warmer foreground colours contrast with the less intense and cooler hues for the distant headland.

Pay equal attention to positive and negative shapes in the scene – the shapes of the rocks as well as the shapes created by sky and sea. It is worth considering the choice of brushes for painting rocks. The essence of rock structures can often be best described by using a flat or filbert brush to achieve some hard-edged, angular brush strokes. I find working in an opaque medium such as oils or pastels more effective than watercolour as it is easier to give a feeling of solidity and shapes can be modified more easily with lighter colours.

Boats and Harbours

For many artists there is nothing more exciting than painting amid the sights and sounds of a bustling harbour. So why do so many painters find the subject so difficult? Perhaps it's because harbours contain too much material. Sorting out a composition from a jumble of boats and buildings, mud and reflections as well as considering the continually changing environment can be daunting no matter what your level of ability.

Keeping it simple

Sorting out the scene with a black and white sketch is where I normally start. It helps me to find the essentials in a subject

◄ In this quick charcoal sketch I also used black and white Conté crayons to add the details.

▼ **Quayside, Dartmouth**
watercolour
13 x 18 cm (5 x 7 in)
A watercolour should portray an impression, a mood and a moment in time. The scene was simply stated by using a limited palette of granulating colours.

and squinting at the scene makes the details disappear so I see just the masses. I often find this invaluable, especially for recording the scene when the tide is on the turn. I apply the same principles of simplifying details when I am working in colour.

Drawing boats

'I can't draw boats!' is something I frequently hear from students on my painting courses. However, it really is no more difficult than drawing anything else. As there are so many different types of boats you will need to do a lot of sketchbook work in order to become familiar with the different lines and shapes.

Measuring and comparison

We tend to draw what we know from experience rather than what we see with our eyes. Therefore, observing both objectively and analytically is something you must learn to do if you wish to improve your marine scenes. Constant checking of proportions and making comparisons is vital and with practice soon becomes automatic. I find the traditional thumb on pencil method of measuring the best way to do this.

Many students get the angles wrong from the outset, thereby often making the boat lean over far too much. Checking the correct angle of the mast, cabin or bow should be the first step. Making boats sit on the mud or on the water is another common difficulty. This is usually because the shadows or reflections are not stated strongly enough, so the boats

tend to float in mid air. With watercolour I often merge a 'wet-into-wet' wash on the keel and into the sand or water, making it difficult to distinguish between the two.

A simple aid

Think of a boat in the shape of a rectangular box, which will also help you with perspective. A boat can be constructed within this shape and proportions can be aided further by adding centre lines between the bow and stern and transom and keel. If the boat has a cabin this is simply another, smaller box on top. Curves must be well observed – students often make these rise far too steeply.

When it comes to rigging and ropes, don't put every one in – just indicate a few major ones, flicked in with a rigger brush or pencil.

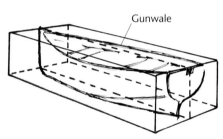

Horizon/eye level

Gunwale

Horizon/eye level

▶ In this pencil sketch the angle of the boat is dictated by the mast and cabin. On location you will find it useful to hold up a pencil to check the angle at which the boat leans. Drawing a vertical line on your paper may also be helpful.

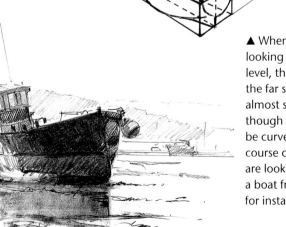

▲ When you are looking at a boat at eye level, the gunwale on the far side will appear almost straight, even though you know it to be curved. This will of course change if you are looking down into a boat from a quay, for instance.

▶ This graphite pencil sketch demonstrates how varying the weight of line can be useful in emphasizing the main focal point of the scene.

Composition

When you are faced with a complicated harbour scene it can often be quite a daunting task to find a simple and satisfying composition. Our eyes take in the broader view, so we tend to think we should include everything we see. This is when you will find a viewfinder invaluable as it helps to isolate a particular subject and focus on what interests you. Placing

▼ Looking *contre-jour* at a scene not only simplifies it but also makes for a far more dramatic picture with strong contrasts of tone, as seen in this quick sketch.

your centre of interest in the Golden Section also helps. This means your focal point lies on one of the four intersections of two imaginary horizontal and vertical lines dividing the picture into thirds.

▶ **Quayside, Looe**
watercolour
25 x 36 cm (10 x 14 in)
The contrasts of sand, reflections and moving water were my main inspiration in this scene. The feeling of movement was achieved by a vigorous painting approach and by using some painterly brushwork.

Arranging the subject

Before starting there are a number of decisions to consider, such as whether to use a portrait or landscape format and a high or low horizon line, the balance of tonal areas and direction of light and where the centre of interest will be. Producing a series of quick thumbnail sketches similar to those shown here gives you a clearer idea in establishing the principal arrangement of a composition and helps you to sort out important priorities before starting a painting. You will soon see how much compositional mileage you can get out of a single viewpoint.

It is rare to find a perfect ready-made scene where the boats are in the ideal position, so be prepared to move them around or leave them out of your picture altogether. Remember not to concentrate entirely upon the boats but also to consider the spaces between them; your aim should be to create a pattern of shapes and tones that will make some interesting negative as well as positive shapes within the picture area.

▲ This photograph of a typical bustling Cornish harbour shows the many problems you are likely to find. The success of a painting means simplifying the scene as much as possible and asking yourself what interests you enough to paint it in the first place.

▲ Because the boat on the right has been cropped it tends to focus the viewer's eye on other two. However, if this boat was moved into the picture to the Golden Section it could easily become the focal point. To highlight this you could use a strong contrast, for instance a bright colour against muted shades or the darkest dark against the lightest light.

◀ Here I have selected two of the boats in the photograph with the most interesting shapes and made the background an important part of the composition. A balance and counterbalance of shapes, including verticals and horizontals, plays a vital part in the overall design.

◀ I like to use an odd number of boats, usually three, often butting one against another. Don't be afraid to crop boats; I often use a stern or bow of a boat to one side to frame the picture or lead the viewer's eye further into it. It creates a sense of space and intrigue and also hints at more beyond the confines of the picture.

▶ Quick sketches provide useful reference for studio paintings later.

▼ **St Ives Harbour**
watercolour and gouache
36 x 55 cm (14 x 21½ in)
The medium of watercolour and gouache on a tinted paper is ideal for dramatic skies and bright sunlight.

Low tide

I love harbours at low tide as they often help to create a much more interesting composition than you find when the tide is in. Tide-pools, wet mud and rusting chains add wonderful contrasts of colour, texture and shape in the painting. By contrast, when the tide is in it can often make for a prettier subject but one that is much more difficult to capture, particularly when you are painting on the spot. Boats bobbing and swinging around on water can be very frustrating, and they may be taken out on a fishing trip before you have finished! I also prefer to see the whole of the boat out of the water, too – the shapes are much more interesting, particularly if the boat is leaning over at an angle.

Adding life

I will often include figures in my paintings, which immediately brings active involvement to a scene and helps bring it to life. Introducing figures can not only give movement, colour and character to a harbour scene, but can also provide a useful scale and narrative content.

Fishermen mending nets on the quay, unloading their catch of fish or repairing boats can be interesting subjects in their own right.

The value of looking hard at figures and their activity and trying to get a few well-observed lines down in your sketchbook cannot be overestimated. Try to capture the overall pose of the figures as quickly as possible and describe their movements and gestures, no matter how brief they are. You will find that squinting will help, as you will see the whole body as a simple shape. If time allows it is also useful to include some of the surroundings in your sketches too. This will help in particular with the relative size of figures to their environment; if they are not in scale in the picture it will be immediately obvious to the viewer.

Wildlife such as seagulls and various waterfowl can also play an important part in suggesting movement and life in a scene. A few flicks of a rigger brush is all that is required in order to indicate some gulls swirling in the sky. Just as with a well-placed figure, they can either form the focal point of a composition or provide a pointer to it by leading the viewer's eye to where they are positioned.

◀ This sketch was done using a 4B pencil and a felt-tip pen. I sometimes combine these pencil sketches with a ballpoint pen and other media too.

▼ **Old Newlyn Harbour**
oils
23 x 33 cm (9 x 13 in)
This old Cornish harbour is always a pleasure to paint, partly for its charm, but also for its association with the fine colony of artists that sprang up here, led by Stanhope Forbes, at the turn of the century.

Sunlit Shallows

*Capturing this fleeting moody moment of ethereal light
on the Exe estuary was my challenge. Watercolour was the
natural choice for a subject such as this. It also provided an ideal
opportunity to use a number of traditional watercolour
techniques in the same painting.*

◀ First stage

Watercolours

Cadmium Orange

Naples Yellow

Raw Sienna

Coeruleum

Phthalo Blue

Permanent Rose

First Stage

For this painting I chose a 300 gsm (140 lb) Whatman paper (Not) that had been previously stretched onto a board with gummed brown-paper tape. I sketched in the main features using a 4B pencil and then applied masking fluid with an old brush to reserve the highlighted areas. This was applied with a light touch in order to pick up the 'tooth' of the paper to suggest the sparkling water. This was then allowed to dry. Using my large hake brush I applied an overall wash of Cadmium Orange mixed with some Naples Yellow and merged this at the same time with a mixture of Coeruleum and Permanent Rose.

Second Stage

When this initial wash was dry I laid a second wet-into-wet wash of the same colours over areas of this, but also added Phthalo Blue to the water to give a stronger contrast. While the paper was still damp I dropped in a mixture of Phthalo Blue and Raw Sienna for the middle distance, the trees and their reflections. I felt now that I had set the required mood and built up a suitable tonal foundation on which to build up the painting further.

◀ Second stage

◀ Third stage

Third Stage

I now rubbed off the masking fluid with my finger to reveal the highlights. This is always an exciting time, as it immediately gives contrast and sparkle to the painting. Using a smaller round brush I applied Raw Sienna to the foreground sand, using a dry-brush technique. The slightly dryer paint now added more contrast as well as texture to the foreground. A further wash was added to the water again to accentuate the sunlight upon it, using a mixture of Coeruleum and Permanent Rose. This same mixture was also applied to the distant hills, as well as a more watered-down mixture to soften some of the edges of the reserved whites in the middle distance.

45

Finished Stage

The final touches were to emphasize the modelling of the boats, as well as adding further details to them without overworking. For the hull of the boat on the left I used a mix of Cadmium Orange and Permanent Rose, adding Phthalo Blue for the keel. Coeruleum and Permanent Rose were used to build up the tones on the other two boats. The masts were painted in with a small rigger, using a ruler to rest the ferrule of the brush on. I added the rigging and ropes by simply using a 4B pencil, taking care not to get too fussy. I also decided to add some life to the scene, so I flicked in some seagulls with a rigger, using Permanent White gouache around the boat, which I had decided was my focal point. A few touches of white gouache were also added to the boats, as well as to the sandbanks.

When I paint in watercolour a quote by the master watercolourist John Varley always springs to mind. He used to tell his pupils, 'A flat wash is like a silence in which you can hear the faintest whisper.'

▶ **Sunlit Shallows, Topsham**
watercolour
25 x 36 cm (10 x 14 in)

Breaking Waves

*Thundering waves crashing onto rugged rocks is
one of the most impressive sights that nature has to offer
and it never ceases to inspire me. I wanted to create a sense of
movement and energy in this painting of the Cornish coast and
to achieve that I decided to work with a combination
of watercolour and soft pastel.*

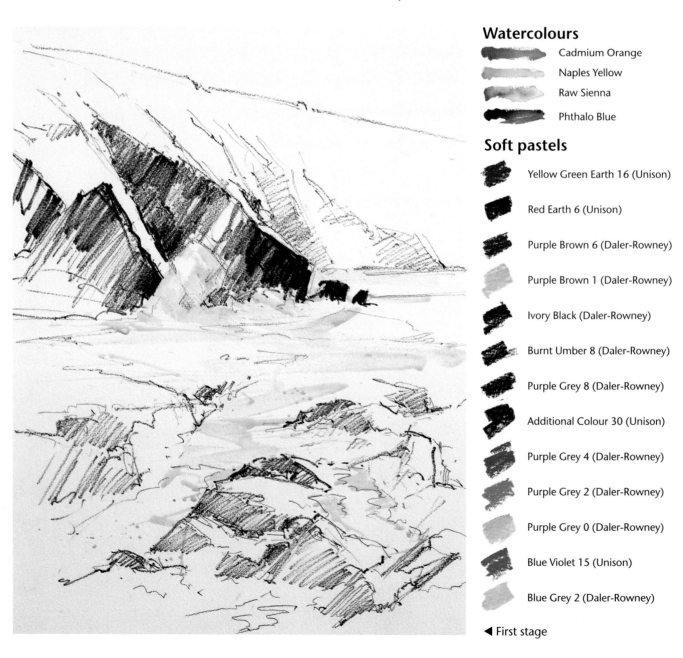

Watercolours

Cadmium Orange

Naples Yellow

Raw Sienna

Phthalo Blue

Soft pastels

Yellow Green Earth 16 (Unison)

Red Earth 6 (Unison)

Purple Brown 6 (Daler-Rowney)

Purple Brown 1 (Daler-Rowney)

Ivory Black (Daler-Rowney)

Burnt Umber 8 (Daler-Rowney)

Purple Grey 8 (Daler-Rowney)

Additional Colour 30 (Unison)

Purple Grey 4 (Daler-Rowney)

Purple Grey 2 (Daler-Rowney)

Purple Grey 0 (Daler-Rowney)

Blue Violet 15 (Unison)

Blue Grey 2 (Daler-Rowney)

◄ First stage

First Stage

For this painting I chose an Arche 300 gsm (140 lb) Not watercolour paper that had been previously stretched onto a board with gummed brown-paper tape. I began work by lightly sketching in the scene using a 4B pencil and then blocked in some dark tones with a black permanent (waterproof) felt-tip pen. This helped me to confirm my ideas for the composition. I reserved the highlights for the breaking waves and surf with the use of masking fluid applied with an old brush, also adding some spattering of it in the foreground.

Second Stage

I now mixed a number of colours together on my palette. These included Cadmium Orange and Naples Yellow, Phthalo Blue and Raw Sienna as well as Phthalo Blue and some watered-down black ink. Working quickly, using my hake brush, I covered the whole of the paper with these mixes, allowing some of the colours to merge together wet-into-wet on the paper.

▶ Third stage

▶ This detail of the third stage shows how depth and recession are achieved by the use of tonal values and warm and cool colours.

Third Stage

When this was dry, using the same mixture of colours, I built up the tonal foundation further. More darks were added to the rocks using a combination of watered-down black ink and a watercolour mixture of Phthalo Blue and Cadmium Orange. At this stage it was important that I did not overwork the transparency of the watercolour in the sea, so I decided that this was best left alone. Instead, I turned my attention to building up further washes on the rocks and headland in order to suggest solidity and contrast.

Fourth Stage

It was now time to remove the masking fluid, which I achieved by rubbing it off with my finger. This immediately added contrast to the painting and although hard edges were inevitable, some of these would be softened with pastel at a later stage in the painting process.

The painting now had a strong foundation on which to add some pastel. When applying pastel it is always best to start with the sky to set the mood. To provide contrast to the subtle glow of yellow in the sky I applied a soft Blue Grey pastel on its side, which I blended with a tissue to soften it further. I also used the same grey for the light catching the edges of the cliffs. A tip to bear in mind: when you have a pastel in your hand, check to see where else you can use it in the picture. Echoing colours in this way will give a unity to the painting.

I added a dark and mid-tone purple in the headland, as well as in the rocks in the foreground, providing a link between the two. The tooth of the paper was useful here as the broken colour gave contrast as well as texture to the picture.

Fifth Stage

I added a light Blue Grey pastel to some of the highlighted areas of the surf, not only to soften the hard edges but also to avoid drawing attention away from the main wave, which was the centre of interest in the picture. To add further depth and to contrast with the cooler hues in the distance, warmer darks were added to the foreground rocks using red/brown pastels.

Finished Stage

All that remained to do now was to add a few finishing touches. I added further highlights to the cliff face using light blue and pink pastels. I also added a grey mixed with Phthalo Blue watercolour and Permanent White gouache for further modelling in the cliff face. I simplified some areas of broken colour produced by the pastel marks by softening with a wet brush and firmed up the shape of the main wave with Permanent White gouache. I also mixed a light colour using Cadmium Orange and Permanent White Gouache, which I used to give form to the rocks in the foreground. Using Yellow Green Earth pastel on its side and applying a downward movement, I suggested a reflection of the cliff in the shallow water. To complete the painting I added a few swirling seagulls with a rigger and Permanent White gouache.

▲ Fifth stage

◀ Foregrounds are best kept simple. This detail of the fifth stage shows how pastel applied lightly on its side suggests texture and form.

▶ **Breaking Waves, Talland Bay**
watercolour and pastel
46 x 33 cm (18 x 13 in)

Sun and Shadows

*The morning shadows set across a Cornish beach
from a high viewpoint made for an interesting composition.
I chose the rich opacity of oils to help capture the interplay
of contrasting shapes and colour.*

Oils

- Cadmium Orange
- Cadmium Yellow
- Raw Sienna
- Naples Yellow
- Cadmium Red
- Rose Madder
- French Ultramarine
- Viridian
- Titanium White

◀ First stage

First Stage

For this painting I used a prepared piece of MDF already primed with two coats of acrylic gesso and a final coat mixed with an equal amount of texture paste. Using a large flat brush, I applied a relatively fluid wash of Cadmium Orange over the entire board. While this was still wet I took the colour back

further by removing it with a rag to leave a uniform mid tone. This was then left to dry. Using a small soft round brush and a 'turpsy' mix of French Ultramarine and Burnt Sienna I lightly sketched in a few constructional lines for the composition, as well as blocking in the cliffs and shadow areas. I also lifted out the main highlights with a rag dipped in white spirit. This now established the foundation of the painting.

Second Stage

The next step was to set the mood of the painting and the sky is the best place to begin. Using a mixture of French Ultramarine, Naples Yellow and Titanium White I painted in the sky, also adding

a slightly warmer mix of French Ultramarine and Rose Madder in some areas. These colours were repeated in the tide-pools and also in the foreground where less white was used in the mixes. I added further darks in the cliffs using a mixture of French Ultramarine and Burnt Sienna. Now was a good time to establish some mid tones to the cliff face and these were added using mixes of French Ultramarine, Cadmium Orange and Titanium White, as well as French Ultramarine, Cadmium Red and Titanium White.

Third Stage

I now worked on the sea with mixes of French Ultramarine and Rose Madder plus Titanium White and French Ultramarine and Viridian plus Titanium White. For the shadows of the cliffs on the beach I used a mixture of French Ultramarine, Cadmium Red and a little Titanium White. I painted this as thinly as possible so the colours beneath would show through and give a variety of colour. I also added a stronger blue for the shadowed water in the foreground using French Ultramarine, Rose Madder and Titanium White.

Finished Stage

On assessing the painting at this stage, I felt that it was necessary for the sky to be linked with the landscape more by adding the same blue that I had used in the tide-pools. This same colour was blended and lightened further as the colour merged with the paint previously applied to give a soft effect. I also added a touch of warmth to the sky by way of the clouds, some of which I blended with my finger.

I now concentrated on the colours to be found in the sunlit areas of the beach. For the lighter sand I used mixes of Cadmium Yellow, Naples Yellow and Titanium White. For the darker sand colours I used mixtures of Raw Sienna, Rose Madder, Cadmium Orange and Titanium White. Some of these colours were also echoed on the sunlit areas of the cliff face. To help the recession, I added further

darks to the foreground rocks using Viridian and French Ultramarine. Finally, I added a few touches of Titanium White for the surf breaking on the rocks, as well as in the tide-pool. All that was now left to do was to add a suggestion of life to the scene. This I did by adding a few swirling seagulls, with a small rigger brush, around the centre of interest.

▲ **Sun and Shadows, Mawgan Porth**
oils
30 x 30 cm (12 x 12 in)

Fishing Boats

A busy harbour with colourful fishing boats such as this view of Polperro in Cornwall is always an exciting prospect. I decided that watercolour and gouache, applied expressively on a tinted support, would help to simplify and unify this complex scene.

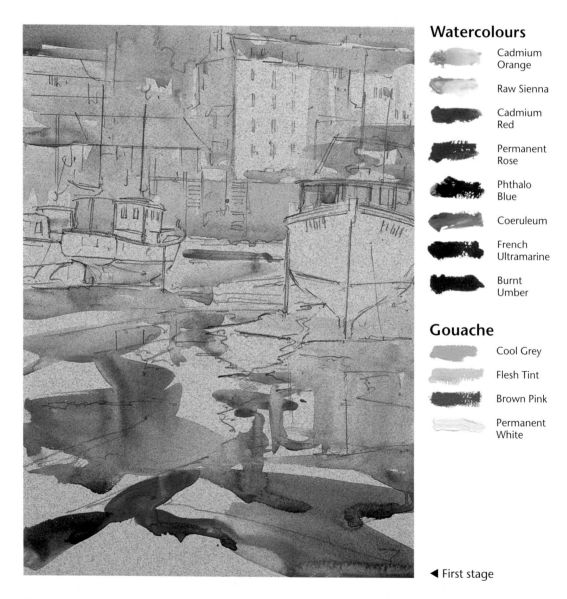

Watercolours

Cadmium Orange

Raw Sienna

Cadmium Red

Permanent Rose

Phthalo Blue

Coeruleum

French Ultramarine

Burnt Umber

Gouache

Cool Grey

Flesh Tint

Brown Pink

Permanent White

◀ First stage

First Stage

For this painting I decided to use a Canson Mi-Teintes pastel paper (colour Moonstone) that I had previously stretched onto a board.

I prefer to use the reverse side of this paper for painting, as it has a less mechanical surface. My initial interest was in the reflections in the tide-pools rather than the

buildings or the fishing boats. Therefore, I decided upon a portrait format with a higher horizon line. I indicated the fishing boats with a 4B pencil, cropping the two on either side of the frame to make a more interesting composition.

Next, I prepared a number of mixes of watercolour on my palette. These were French Ultramarine and Cadmium Orange, French Ultramarine and Raw Sienna, and Coeruleum and Permanent Rose. I merged these washes together on the paper using my large hake brush and also added a touch of Brown Pink gouache for the foreground. It was important that I left some of the original paper untouched in order to add a unity to the painting.

Second Stage

When this was dry I decided to apply some dark colours. For the keels of the boats I used Phthalo Blue and Cadmium Red. I also added a further wash using a mixture of Coeruleum and Raw Sienna for the distant trees, harbour wall and foreground. For the cabin of the boat I used a mixture of Burnt Umber with a touch of French Ultramarine, which I also applied in the shadows below the boats and chains in the foreground. For the sunlit keel and gunwale of the larger fishing boat I used Coeruleum.

Third Stage

Having now established my darks I decided that it was time to add the lights in order to help assess the mid tones. For this I used a thicker and dryer mix of Permanent White gouache, which was added to the bright sunlit areas of the boats and buildings. At the same time I added a diluted 'milky' wash to the buildings and reflections. I mixed a touch of Coeruleum watercolour to the Permanent White gouache and dry-brushed this quickly into the harbour mud to suggest water.

◀ In this detail of the third stage you can see the highlights created with Permanent White gouache.

▶ Fourth stage

Fourth Stage

For the shadows throughout the picture
I used a warm mixture of French Ultramarine
and Cadmium Red with a touch of Permanent
White gouache. In order to suggest the
reflected light on the hull of the large fishing
boat, it was important that the colour was
applied thinly, allowing some of the colour
of the paper to show through the wash. I had
decided that the red fishing boat to the left was
to be the centre of interest and for this I used
Cadmium Red. For the stern in shadow,
I added a further wash of French Ultramarine.

◀ In this detail of the
fourth stage the
colours used for the
shadow areas were
kept on the warm side
to suggest the bright
summer's day.

61

gouache. Finally, all that was left for me to do was to add the finishing touches with a smaller brush. These included the details of the boats, for which I used a rigger and small round brush. A few further lights were added, including a mixture of Raw Sienna and Permanent White gouache, and finally the ropes and rigging were applied with the use of a 4B pencil.

Conclusion

There is no doubt that just being beside water is an enjoyable and inspirational experience, whether it is by a busy harbour, quiet estuary or wild open sea. I hope you have enjoyed this brief insight into some of these aspects. However, the main purpose of this book has been not only to show you how I work, but also to arouse your own enthusiasm for a subject with unlimited possibilities. Painting coastal landscapes is a subject that I am passionate about and I hope I have succeeded in passing on to you some encouragement and useful ideas that you can incorporate into your own work. One of the most important qualities in painting is personal interpretation so, above all else, be sure to express your own emotions about the subject using the sensitivity of your chosen medium.

Fifth Stage
I continued to work up the tonal foundation of the picture, taking care that no particular area became too detailed. It was important to keep the background as simple as possible otherwise the whole picture would be too complicated. In this part of the painting I added Cool Grey gouache to the roofs of the buildings and harbour wall as well as some further dark tones.

Finished Stage
I decided to add texture to the foreground by spattering a mixture of French Ultramarine and Cadmium Red with a bristle brush. Some warmer lights were also added to the foreground with touches of Flesh Tint

▶ **Fishing Boats, Polperro Harbour**
watercolour and gouache
34 x 25 cm (13 x 9½ in)

⟡ Collins

THE NEXT STEP...

If you have enjoyed this book, why not have a look at other art instruction titles from Collins?

Other titles in the *Learn to Paint* series include:

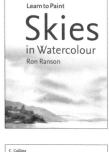
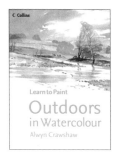
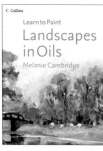

And if you want to take your painting further, try these titles:

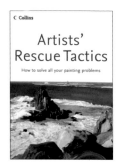
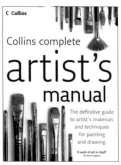

To order any of these titles, please telephone **0870 787 1732**
For further information about Collins books, visit our website:
www.collins.co.uk

Some other addresses and websites you might find useful are:

ART MAGAZINES
The Artist, Caxton House, 63/65 High Street, Tenterden, Kent TN30 6BD; tel: 01580 763673
www.theartistmagazine.co.uk
Artists & Illustrators, The Fitzpatrick Building, 188-194 York Way, London N7 9QR; tel: 020 7700 8500
Leisure Painter, Caxton House, 63/65 High Street, Tenterden, Kent TN30 6BD; tel: 01580 763315
www.leisurepainter.co.uk

ART MATERIALS
Daler-Rowney Ltd, Bracknell, Berkshire RG12 8ST; tel: 01344 424621
www.daler-rowney.com
Winsor & Newton, Whitefriars Avenue, Wealdstone, Harrow, Middlesex HA3 5RH; tel: 020 8427 4343
www.winsornewton.com

ART SOCIETIES
Society for All Artists (SAA), P. O. Box 50, Newark, Nottinghamshire NG23 5GY; tel: 01949 844050
www.saa.co.uk

BOOKCLUBS
Artists' Choice, P. O. Box 3, Huntingdon, Cambridgeshire PE28 0QX; tel: 01832 710201
www.artists-choice.co.uk

INTERNET RESOURCES
Artcourses: an easy way to find part-time classes, workshops and painting holidays
www.artcourses.co.uk
Painters Online: interactive art club run by The Artist's Publishing Company
www.painters-online.com
Ray Balkwill: the author's website, with details of his courses, exhibitions and a gallery of his paintings
www.raybalkwill.co.uk

VIDEOS
APV Films, 6 Alexandra Square, Chipping Norton, Oxfordshire OX7 5HL; tel: 01608 641798
www.apvfilms.com

Teaching Art, P. O. Box 50, Newark, Nottinghamshire NG23 5GY; tel: 01949 844050
www.teachingart.com